Cake
Decorating

Lorraine Sorby-Howlett
&
Marian Jones

C&A CHILD &
ASSOCIATES
AN ALL-AUSTRALIAN PUBLISHER

Published by
Child & Associates Publishing Pty Ltd,
9 Clearview Place, Brookvale, NSW, Australia, 2100
A wholly owned Australian publishing company
This book has been edited, designed and typeset
in Australia by the Publisher
Co-published in the U.K. and North America by
Merehurst Press, 5 Great James Street,
London, WC1N 3DA

First Edition 1987

© Lorraine Sorby-Howlett, Marian Jones 1987

Photography by Lennart Osbeck

Printed in Singapore by Tien Wah Press Pte Ltd

National Library of Australia Cataloguing-in-Publication

Sorby-Howlett, Lorraine, 1940-
Birthday designs.

ISBN 0 86777 307 3.

1. Cake decorating. I. Jones, Marian, 1938-
II. Title.

641.8'653

Contents

INTRODUCTION

I met Marian Jones and Lorraine Sorby-Howlett many years ago and because of our common interest in cake decorating, we have become very close friends.

After the huge success of their first book *Wedding Designs*, Marian and Lorraine have combined again to publish their ideas on birthday cakes.

How often we hear the call for a simple cake and our minds go into neutral, especially if it is a design for the man of the house (little or big). With their simple side borders and designs this collection will be most welcomed by decorators, especially those who like to produce attractive cakes but are not able to tackle show creations with their complicated decorations. This book will be an invaluable reference for the beginner as well as the advanced decorator.

I am proud to recommend these two dedicated ladies and their book and I wish them every success with this publication.

MARGARET LENANE
CANBERRA

EBONY LACE

Dramatic colours have been used on this unusual cake. The colour scheme is softened by the double frills as well as the delicately tinted roses combined with orange blossom and maidenhair fern.

Lace pattern shown actual size

You will need:

To bake	1 medium oval cake
Board	allow 5 cm (2 inch) larger all round than cake
Flowers	1 large rose 6 small roses 7 orange blossom 4 sprays of baby's breath 4 sprigs of maidenhair fern
Ribbons	5 bunches of loops

GROWING UP

This cake will appeal to the very special young lady. The softness of the lace frames a delightful flooded scene and to personalise the cake the medallion has the lady's initials.

You will need:

To bake	1 medium oval cake
Board	allow 5 cm (2 inch) larger all round than cake
Flowers	21 small cutter flowers

CHOCOLATE TWIST

Browns and lemons combine well with the royal icing flooded board to give this simple cake an elegant look.

Pattern shown half-size

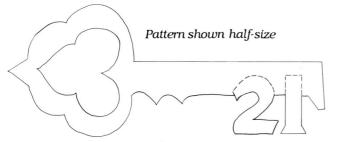

You will need:

To bake	23 x 18 cm (9 x 7 inch) oblong cake
Board	30 x 23 cm (12 x 9 inch) oblong
Flowers	12 daisies 6 gumnuts 6 sprays of boronia 12 leaves
Ribbons	7 bunches 1 metre (1 yard) of royal brown velvet

SUMMER DELIGHT

Brush floodwork is the feature of this cake. Frangipanis and tiny blossoms complete the design.

You will need:

To bake   1 medium blossom-shaped cake cut to a fan shape

Board   allow 7.5 cm (3 inch) larger all round than cake

Flowers	10 frangipanis
	11 small blossoms
	10 leaves
Ribbons	6 small bunches

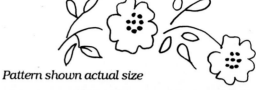

Pattern shown actual size

GOLDEN DAFFODILS

Frills, flounces and lace team well with the golden daffodils on this eye-catching beauty. The lace handkerchief can be embroidered to add a personal touch.

You will need:

To bake	1 medium octagonal cake
Board	allow 5 cm (2 inch) larger all round than cake
Flowers	4 daffodils 4 bunches of boronia 8 leaves
Ribbons	3 bunches

TOP SCORE

The soccer scene has been used on this masculine cake. Your favourite team colours could be used on the guernseys and in the surrounds of the painting.

You will need:

To bake	23 cm (9 inch) round cake
Board	30 cm (12 inch) round

LITTLE DARLING

For that very special first birthday what could be more appropriate than a cake shaped as the figure one. The decoration has been kept simple to allow the tiny doll to be seen at its best.

You will need:

To bake	23 x 18 cm (9 x 7 inch) oblong cake cut to shape
Board	28 x 20 cm (11 x 8 inch) oblong
Flowers	8 rosebuds 8 gentians 30 cutter flowers
Ribbons	4 small bunches
Special Effect:	1 moulded doll

CHOO CHOO CAKE

A delightful cake for that special little boy. The moulded trains have been painted with bright colours and the carriages have a candle for each birthday year.

You will need:

To bake	23 cm (9 inch) round cake
Board	30 cm (12 inch) round

Special Effects: Five small trains comprised of one engine and three carriages for the cake base. One larger engine and carriages for top decoration.

WATTLE THEME

This cake features the unusual green of native wattle. The finish of the board has been carried through in the base leaves and decoration. The sepia tones of the bird have been achieved by using cocoa butter.

Pattern shown actual size

You will need:

To bake	1 key cake
Board	allow 5 cm (2 inch) larger all round than cake
Flowers	38 sprigs of wattle 59 leaves

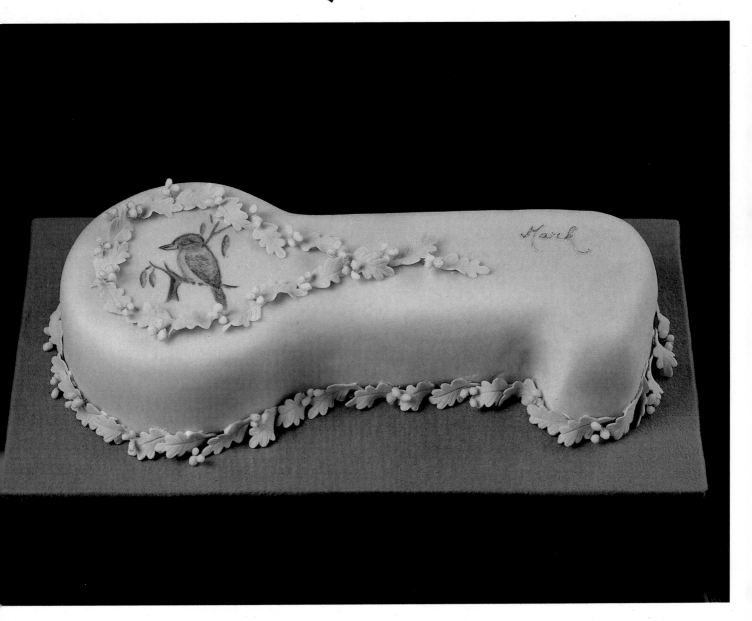

TEE OFF

A twenty-first birthday cake with a difference. The green which has been made of coconut, is surrounded by a small picket fence and the clubs and bag have been moulded. The key was purchased.

You will need:

To bake	23 cm (9 inch) square
Board	30 cm (12 inch) squar
Ribbons	1 metre (1 yard) of 3 wide ribbon, specia base design

SPECIAL DAY

This dainty cake features a flooded centre piece with lace scallops emphasising the octagonal shape of the cake.

50

Pattern shown half size

You will need:

To bake	23 cm (9 inch) octagonal cake
Board	allow 5 cm (2 inch) larger all round than cake
Flowers	8 rosebuds
	5 roses
	5 leaves
	9 bunches of sweet rocket
	8 rosebuds used in embroidery

PLAYTIME

This cake is very suitable for a young child's birthday. The bright colour scheme will attract any youngster. The blocks have been covered in the traditional royal icing method to achieve the smooth finish.

You will need:

To bake	20 cm (8 inch) square cake, 10 cm (4 inch) deep, cut into two 10 cm (4 inch) blocks
Board	25 x 30 cm (10 x 12 inch) oblong

Alternative method:
Bake cakes in two 20 x 10 cm (8 x 4 inch) loaf tins

PINK HAPPINESS

Soft delicate musk tones have been used on this elegant cake. The embroidery and extension work have been kept simple so that the beautiful carnations may be admired.

You will need:

To bake	1 long oval cake
Board	allow 5 cm (2 inch) larger all round than cake
Flowers	7 pixie carnations 17 *Kurume* azaleas 5 mini blossoms 8 leaves
Ribbons	10 bunches

VINTAGE CAR

A technique of chocolate and jelly work gives the unusual effect to the vintage car. The keys have been moulded from modelling paste and hand painted. A good design for a man's cake.

You will need:

To bake	30 cm (12 inch) long oval cake
Board	allow 5 cm (2 inch) larger all round than cake

SKIPPY

This cake has an Australian theme. Although the airbrush technique was used on the kangaroo's head, the same effect could be achieved by using either brush painting or chalks. The design has been kept simple by the use of flannel flowers and ribbon only.

You will need:

To bake   23 cm (9 inch) round cake

Board   30 cm (12 inch) round

Flowers   12 flannel flowers

Ribbons   6 bunches

Pattern shown half-size

SWEET MARIA

A very dainty cake using the broderie anglaise effect in the embroidery. The delicate lace edging frames the lovely orchids and *Bouvardia* has been added for contrast.

You will need:

To bake	23 cm (9 inch) square cake
Board	30 cm (12 inch) square
Flowers	3 orchids 8 Mexican orange blossoms 12 sprays of *Bouvardia*
Ribbons	4 bunches

BURGUNDY SILK

A simple cake featuring a frilled edge and cutter flowers. Air brushing has been used to achieve the very special colouring. The spray of flowers has been wired into a corsage that can be removed and kept.

You will need:

To bake	23 cm (9 inch) round cake
Board	30 cm (12 inch) round
Flowers	9 cutter orchids 5 bunches of *Abelia* bells 11 leaves
Ribbons	4 bunches, 2 with long tails
Special Effect:	60 frilled medallions

Medallion pattern shown actual size

LIFE BEGINS AT FORTY

The beautifully moulded and hand painted duck teams well with the simplicity of the bullrushes and scroll to make this a different cake for that special occasion.

You will need:

To bake	1 medium corner cut diamond cake
Board	allow 5 cm (2 inch) larger around than cake
Special Effects:	6 clusters of bullrushes 1 scroll 1 duck

SWEET WISHES

The scalloped oval shape of the cake has been used to show off the lovely lace and ribbon work and the simple sweet pea sprays. The finishing touch is the greeting card which can carry any verse.

You will need:

To bake	1 medium four-scalloped oval cake
Board	5 cm (2 inch) larger all round than cake
Flowers	2 sprays of sweet peas 2 sprays of tiny blossoms
Ribbons	1 metre (1 yard)

PRETTY BUTTERFLY

The butterfly is the main attraction of this cake which is suspended on small pillars to achieve a light effect under the elaborate flower arrangement.

You will need:

To bake	1 oblong cake
Board	allow 5 cm (2 inch) larger all round than cake

Flowers	6 geraniums
	5 small geraniums
	6 sprays of moulded blossom with buds
	88 large cutter daisies
	64 medium cutter daisies
	36 small cutter daisies
	6 moulded leaves
	numerous piped leaves
Ribbons	6 small bunches
Special Effect:	Butterfly made using lacelon, modelling paste and flooded wings

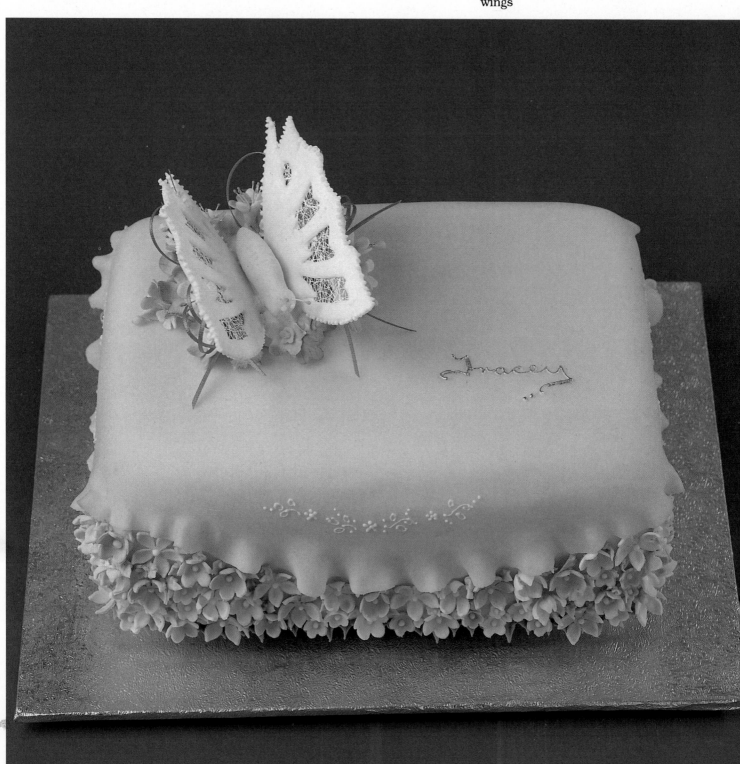

MY PRINCESS

What little girl would not fall in love with this birthday cake. Her ball gown has been finished off with layers of piped tulle lace and ribbon making her pretty enough to be in any enchanted castle.

You will need:

To bake	1 small Dolly Varden cake
Board	30 cm (12 inch) oval
Flowers	9 tiny forget-me-nots
	9 piped leaves
Ribbons	3 metres (3 yards)
Special Effect:	You will need to purchase 1 doll to suit

AUTUMN LEAVES

A special celebration cake in autumn tones. The decoration includes piped grapes and moulded leaves.

You will need:

To bake	1 key cake
Board	allow 5 cm (2 inch) larger all round than cake
Flowers	18 bunches of grapes in varying sizes 18 leaves

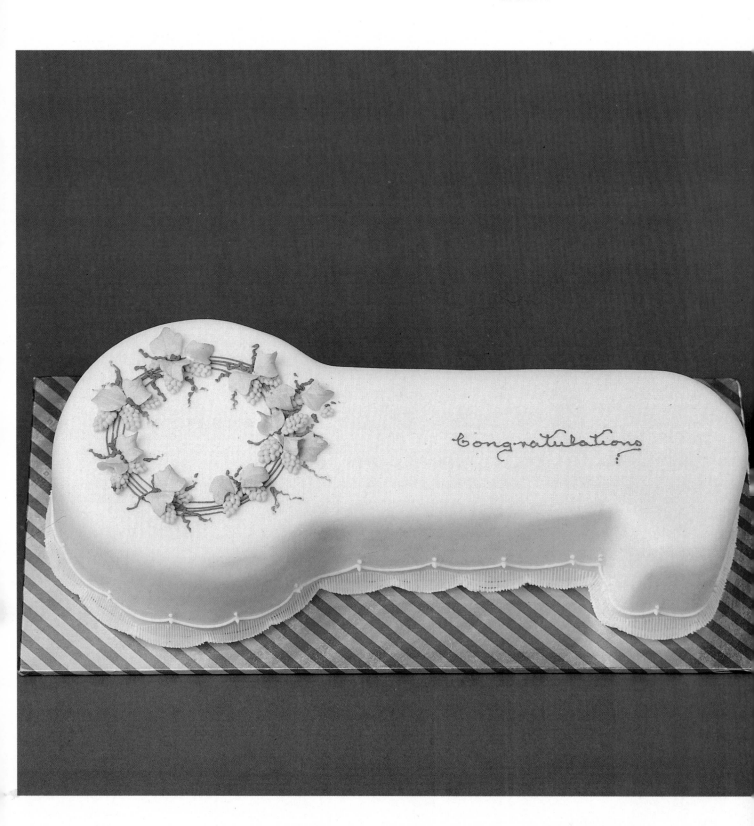

BIRTHDAY MELODY

A very masculine cake with a striking colour scheme dominated by Australian flowers.

You will need:

To bake	1 medium oblong cake with the corners cut
Board	allow 5 cm (2 inch) larger all round than cake
Flowers	17 *Clerodendrum tomentosum* seedpods 1 bud
Ribbons	12 bunches 1 metre (1 yard) for sides
Special Effect:	1 moulded violin

LILAC TIME

A pretty cake with rosebuds and sweet peas combined to make a delightful bouquet.

You will need:

To bake	1 medium oval cake
Board	allow 5 cm (2 inch) larger all round than cake

Flowers	9 sweet peas
	5 rosebuds
	6 leaves
	5 sprays of sweet rocket
	6 bunches of sea lavender
	5 sprays of baby's breath
Ribbons	2 bunches with long tails
	3 bunches with short tails
Special Effect:	60 cutter flowers used in embroidery design

TIFFANY

The beautiful rose is the outstanding feature of this cake. The cake combines two techniques of piping and royal icing floodwork in the attractive side design.

You will need:

To bake	1 medium hexagonal cake
Board	allow 5 cm (2 inch) larger all round than cake
Flowers	1 tiffany rose
	3 half buds
	3 small buds
	5 small blossoms
Ribbons	2 bunches of large loops

DOWN TO THE SEA

The nautical theme of this design is carried through to the royal icing flooded board. To achieve the three dimensional effect the sail has been moulded in gum paste.

You will need:

To bake	23 cm (9 inch) square cake
Board	30 cm (12 inch) square

COMING OF AGE

This cake is for that very special birthday party. The tiered effect allows for the cake size to be varied according to the number of guests. This would be a delightful cake in any colour combination.

You will need:

To bake	2 x 20 cm (8 inch) square cakes
Board	2 x 28 cm (11 inch) square
Flowers	10 carnations 24 mini orchids
Ribbons	10 bunches
Special Effect:	Large silver key 1 metre (1 yard) velvet ribbon 15 cm (6 inch) acrylic pillar

TREASURE CHEST

If your little one would like to become a pirate this the cake for him. It will most certainly catch the children's eyes with the chest full of chocolate coins.

You will need:

To bake	1 loaf tin cake
Board	28 x 15 cm (11 x 6 inch) oblong
Special Effect:	Chocolate coins

CRESCENT MOON

A most unusual cake design. The cakes were sculptured to the crescent shapes, leaving one slightly higher than the other. A simple cascade of flowers was used to emphasise the unusual shape.

You will need:

To bake	23 cm (9 inch) ring cake
Board	36 cm (15 inch) oval
Flowers	34 mountain primula 19 white jasmine
Ribbons	6 bunches

APRICOT ICE

The unusual shape of the key is complemented by the
spray of wired flowers, which has one large *Cattleya*
orchid as the focal point. The beautiful double frill
flounce is enhanced with ribbon and scalloped
medallions.

You will need:

To bake	1 scalloped end key cake
Board	allow 5 cm (2 inch) larger all round than cake

Flowers	1 *Cattleya* orchid
	11 star flowers
	6 buds
	10 sprays
	14 leaves
	baby's breath
	1 butterfly
Ribbons	3 metres (3 yards)
Special Effect:	33 scalloped medallions

This beautiful Cattleya orchid has been hand-moulded and delicately shaded to complete the floral display.

CIRCUS PARADE

To delight the small boy this colourful cake features a birthday clown on the top. The figure clowns on the board can be piped in any position in royal icing.

You will need:

To bake	20 cm (8 inch) square cake
Board	28 cm (11 inch) square
Flowers	6 small cutter flowers
Ribbons	1 1/2 metres (1 1/2 yards) to edge the board
Special Effect:	9 balls in various sizes

Pattern shown half-size

ORCHID FIESTA

This scalloped oval cake is shown off to advantage with a trail of *Phalaenopsis* orchids. The interesting side edge is a combination of icing frills, extension and lace work, which all team well with the ribbon insertion.

You will need:

To bake	1 large scalloped oval cake
Board	allow 5 cm (2 inch) larger all round than cake
Flowers	5 *Phalaenopsis* orchids 12 sprays of star flowers 8 ivy leaves
Ribbons	1 metre (1 yard)

IN THE ROUGH

A masculine cake suitable for any age group. The tree is the main feature of this design.

You will need:

To bake	1 medium oval cake
Board	allow 5 cm (2 inch) larger all round than cake
Ribbons	1 metre (1 yard) for lower edge of cake

THIRSTY DAY

A tankard of beer for the male member of your family. The cork board has been finished with just a few ears of wheat making this an ideal cake for the novice decorator.

You will need:

To bake	15 cm (6 inch) high cylinder cake
Board	20 cm (8 inch) board
Flowers	5 ears of wheat 1 edelweiss
Ribbons	1 bunch

ZODIAC WISHES

A dramatically different approach to the zodiac birthday cake. The crescent moon is set in a beautiful floral arrangement, with the piped star signs scattered among the stars.

You will need:

To bake	1 medium fan-shaped cake
	1 round cake sculptured to a crescent shape
Board	5 cm (2 inch) larger all round
	than cake
Flowers	3 carnations
	2 bunches of spring star blossom
	2 sprays of calico bush
	3 ivy leaves

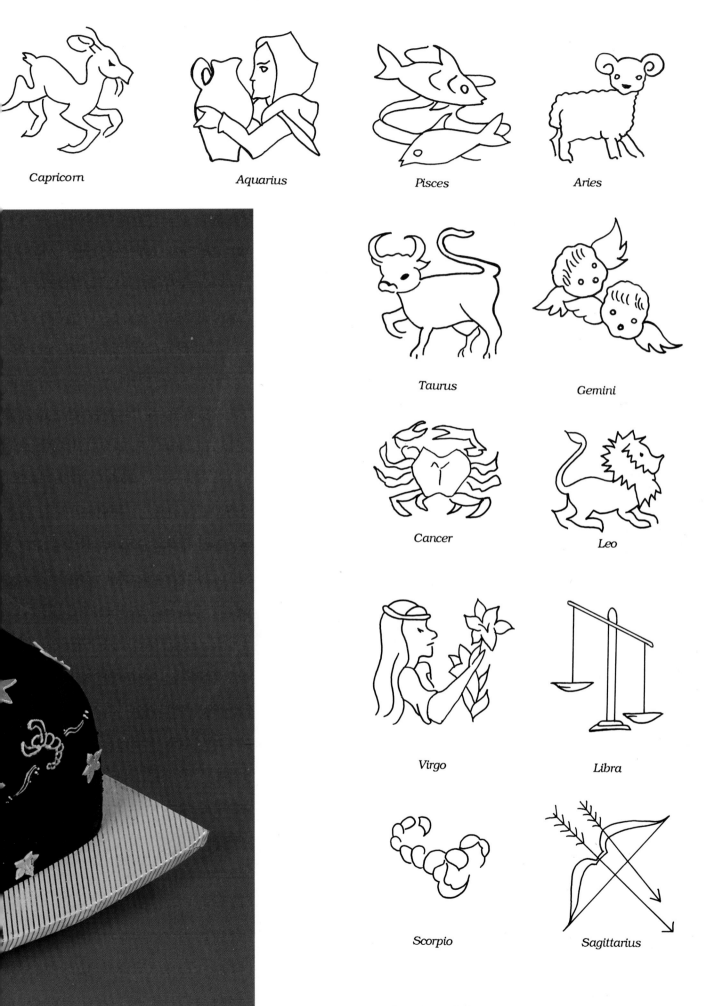

Capricorn

Aquarius

Pisces

Aries

Taurus

Gemini

Cancer

Leo

Virgo

Libra

Scorpio

Sagittarius

These star signs are shown actual size

THE WINNER

This cake is bound to be a winner. The beige and olive colour scheme enhances the wildflower arrangement. The focal point is a moulded horseshoe and horse's head.

You will need:

To bake	1 medium horseshoe cake
Board	allow 4 cm (1 1/2 inch) larger all round than cake
Flowers	1 banksia 3 heads of wheat 8 flowering gum 3 wattle 4 boronia
Ribbons	1 1/2 metres (1 1/2 yards) cut to shape

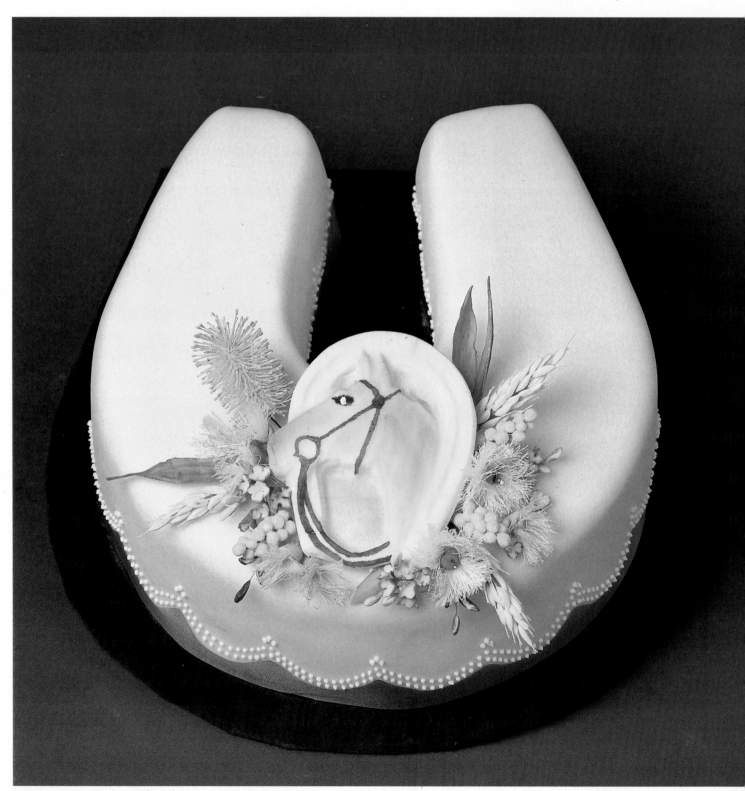

45

TWENTY-ONE

This large cake is very appropriate for that special celebration. The decoration has been kept simple to emphasise the specially shaped cakes.

You will need:

To bake	2 cakes in specially made tins
Board	45 cm (18 inch) square
Flowers	30 bunches of wattle 40 leaves
Ribbons	1 metre (1 yard)

WILDFLOWER WISHES

An unusual cake using flowering gum, boronia and wattle in a horseshoe arrangement. The special board effect was created by cutting medallions from modelling paste and attaching them directly to the board.

You will need:

To bake	1 medium hexagonal cake
Boards	allow 7.5 cm (3 inch) larger all round than cake

Flowers	7 full flowering gums
	7 half flowering gums
	4 sprigs of wattle
	9 sprigs of boronia
	5 leaves
Ribbons	7 bunches
	1 metre (1 yard) for the base of the cake.
Special Effect:	24 medallions needed for the base of the cake .

BOBO THE BIRTHDAY CLOWN

This cake would take pride of place on any birthday table. Clowns should always be in bright colours to attract the eye of that special birthday person.

You will need:

To bake	1 medium oblong cake sculptured to shap (see pattern)
Board	large enough to take clown
Flowers	1 small spray for hat
Ribbons	1 bow for necktie

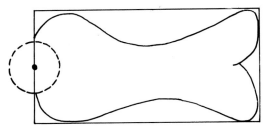

Oblong cake showing cutting lines for the clown's body.

Special Note: To sculpture the cake take a sharp knife and gently cut it into a body shape. Use fondant to make legs and arms and attach them to the cake before placing the clothes. The head is secured with a wooden skewer.

YOUNG AND SWEET

A simple design using cutter flowers in various colour tones. This design would be delightful in any shade.

You will need:

To bake	1 key cake
Board	allow 7.5 cm (3 inch) larger all round than cake
Flowers	54 large cutter flowers 90 small cutter flowers

MY DARLING

This cake is just perfect for that little one's very special day. Soft delicate shades have been used in the floodwork and the exquisite tiny flowers have been specially moulded.

You will need:

To bake	1 medium hexagonal cake
Board	allow 5 cm (2 inch) larger all round than cake
Flowers	12 beauty bush blossoms 8 buds 8 weeping spring cherry blossoms 11 buds 3 leaves

50

WITH LOVE

Beautiful colours blend superbly on this cake which has brush floodwork on the side panels. The board is flooded with royal icing and finished off with a single row of modelling paste medallions.

You will need:

To bake	23 cm (9 inch) round cake
Board	30 cm (12 inch) round
Flowers	24 mountain primulas 14 sprays of sweet rocket 12 leaves 2 birds
Ribbons	9 bunches
Special Effect:	24 medallions for the base edge

'ORM

especially for that person who loves to icing collar, which has been laid flat to cover of the book, can be detached and

You will need:

To bake	1 oblong cake
Board	allow 5 cm (2 inch) larger all round than cake
Flowers	4 pansies

FRAGRANT SHELL

The hand moulded clam shell is filled with the magical water lily tulipa flowers. The shell can be easily removed and kept as a memento of the occasion. The lovely shaded effect has been achieved by lightly dusting the cake with blue petal dust before attaching the shell.

You will need:

To bake	1 medium hexagonal cake
Boards	allow 5 cm (2 inch) larger all round than cake
Flowers	8 water lily tulipa 8 snow-in-the-summer blossoms
Ribbons	5 small loops 2 metres (2 yards) for side banding

SURFRIDER

This cake will appeal to the surfing enthusiast. The design has been put onto the cake using the royal icing painting technique and finished off with moulded sea shells.

You will need:

To bake	23 x 15 cm (9 x 6 inch) oblong cake
Board	30 x 25 cm (12 x 10 inch) oblong
Special Effect:	7 shells of varying sizes have been made from modelling paste

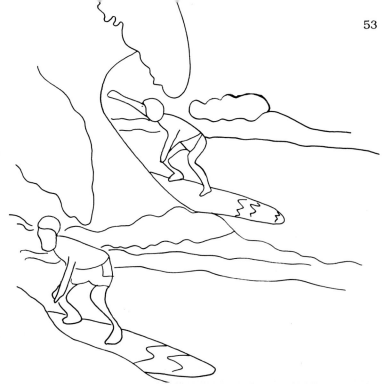

Pattern shown three-quarter size

54

OLDE WORLDE

The edge design on this cake features medallions, ribbon and tiny cutter flowers. The colour scheme of the pansies is echoed in the medallions.

You will need:

To bake	20 cm (8 inch) square cake
Board	28 cm (11 inch) square
Flowers	4 pansies 4 bunches of sweet rocket 5 leaves 10 small blossoms 32 cutter flower
Ribbons	3 small bunches
Special Effect:	48 medallions for base edge

SOFT MIST

The striking ribbon effect on the top of this cake is offset by the subtle shading in the floral arrangement. Delicate embroidery and lace adorn the sides of the cake which is finished off with a royal icing board.

You will need:

To bake	1 medium oval cake
Board	flooded 5 cm (2 inch) larger all round than cake
Flowers	9 peonies 9 bunches of *Marianthus* flowers
Ribbons	3 medium loops—two toned
Special Effect:	The board is edged with velvet ribbon

LAVENDER FAN

Ideal for any birthday, the fan is delicately tinted after moulding and is shown off to best advantage by the use of a single flower and leaves.

You will need:

To bake	20 cm (8 inch) square cake
Board	28 cm (11 inch) square
Flowers	1 *Gordonia* 1 bud 7 leaves
Ribbons	1 single loop

SWEET SIXTEEN

Soft delicate colours have been used in this sweet pretty cake for the teenager. The girl has been moulded in the three dimensional method, and the floral work kept very simple.

You will need:

To bake	1 medium corner cut oblong cake
Board	allow 7.5 cm (3 inch) larger all round than cake
Flowers	17 large cutter daisies 27 tiny cutter daisies
Ribbons	1 metre (1 yard) velvet

58

HAPPY RETURNS

Dainty lace in a zigzag pattern around the cake and delicate embroidery are shown off to perfection in this pretty birthday cake. Orchids and fairy bells are the main flowers in the floral arrangement.

You will need:

To bake	1 medium octagonal cake
Board	allow 5 cm (2 inch) larger all round than cake
Flowers	7 *Dendrobium* orchids 14 fairy bells 6 single sweet rocket 6 sprays of baby's breath
Ribbons	5 bunches of loops

RING OF ROSES

Flounces, dogwood roses and sweet rocket team well on this cake. The cake has been specially baked in a ring tin and would be delightful in any colour shading.

You will need:

To bake	23 cm (9 inch) ring cake
Board	30 cm (12 inch) round
Flowers	11 dogwood roses
	12 bunches of sweet rocket
	11 leaves
Ribbons	11 small bunches

CELEBRATION TIME

This beautiful cake is just perfect for that grand celebration. The mountain primula and small flowers cascade from the tapers to the base board then flow towards the centre to highlight the important 100.

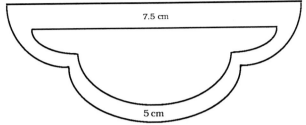

You will need:

To bake	1 large scalloped oval cake, cut in two
Board	allow 5 cm (2 inch) larger than cake on front and 7.5 cm (3 inch) on back *(see below)*
Flowers	75 mountain primulas 12 bunches of sweet rocket 20 snow-in-the-summer
Ribbons	10 bunches of loops
Special Effect:	3 x 7.5 cm (3 inch) pillars on the back board supporting the top cake 3 tapers

MERRY-GO-ROUND

With its charming painted carousel this cake would be suitable for a boy or girl. The sidework has been kept simple to emphasise the carousel.

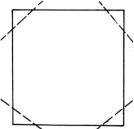

You will need:

To bake	25 cm (10 inch) square cake with corners cut
Board	30 cm (12 inch) board with corners cut
Flowers	11 mountain primula 10 star flowers 5 wild violets 5 leaves 3 spring blossom 7 mini flowers
Ribbons	1 large bunch of long tails

RUBY RED

Adorning the top of this cake is a Victorian posy of red roses and small blossoms. The cake is finished with an insertion of red ribbon and ruby red foil on the board.

You will need:

To bake	20 cm (8 inch) square cake
Board	28 cm (11 inch) square
Flowers	7 red roses 5 Mexican orange blossoms 3 sprays of sweet rocket 8 leaves
Ribbons	1 long loop 50 cm (18 inch) for insertion work